BLACK RELIGIOSITY:

A BIBLICAL AND HISTORICAL PERSPECTIVE

E. G. SHERMAN JR., PHD, D.S.T., D.A.

Black Religiosity: A Biblical and Historical Perspective
Copyright © 2022 by E. G. Sherman Jr., PhD, D.S.T., D.A.

All rights reserved. No part of this book may be reproduced or transmitted in any form or by any means, electronic or mechanical, including photocopying, recording, or by any information storage and retrieval system without express written permission from the author, except in the case of brief quotations embodied in critical reviews and certain other noncommercial uses permitted by copyright law.

Printed in the United States of America.

Brilliant Books Literary
137 Forest Park Lane Thomasville
North Carolina 27360 USA

TABLE OF CONTENTS

Dedication v
This Book Salutes Events In vii
Acknowledgment ix
Preface xi
Introduction xiii

What Is Man? 1
The Slaves' Religious Experiences 5
The Ethiopian Eunuch 9
An Outreach Legacy of a Black Church 13
The Saga of Black Preaching in America 17
Chasing the Mirage of Equality 22
The American Black Dilemma 28

Epilogue 35
Suggested Readings 37
About the Author 39

DEDICATION

This booklet is dedicated to memories of Dr. Dolores E. Sherman who departed to be with the Lord December 15, 2008 after thirty-nine years of blissful marriage and, secondly, included are members of Institutional First Baptist Church where I am founding pastor and continuing to serve during the past forty one years; students of the Albany Extension of Bethany Divinity College and Seminary in Dothan, Alabama; and readers of my sermons posted as www.biblicalechoes.com since June of 2007.

THIS BOOK SALUTES EVENTS IN

January

    1. Emancipation Day, January 1, 1863
    2. Martin Luther King, Jr's Birthday—Jan 15
    3. Inauguration of President Obama—Jan 21

February

    1. President Lincoln's birthday—Feb 12
    2. Frederick Douglass' birthday—Feb 20
    3. Carter G. Woodson started Negro History Week—2nd week in February
    4. Black History Month—February

ACKNOWLEDGMENT

Words of appreciation are extended to our church members and readers of my posted sermons who continue to request a bound copy of sermons. I mentioned this recurring request to my sister, Dr. Mary E. Benjamin, Vice President for Academic Affairs at the University at Pine Bluff, Ark and she expressed a similar interest. However, she ventured further and agreed to assist in a publication undertaking. I was both honored and challenged by her encouraged. "Sis" Thanks.

Eugene G. Sherman, Jr.

PREFACE

This booklet is a compilation of several sermons undergirded by the common theme of Black Religiosity in America. It makes no attempt to provide an extensive history of the religious stages and/or development in the African-American arena. Instead, it focuses on eclectic religious experiences of this population.

As noted in this document, the Afro-American religious experiences predated slavery even though some apologists claim that the former Africans were introduced to Christianity through the system of slavery. This claim will be refuted in the sermon on The Ethiopian Eunuch contained in this booklet.

Lastly, this book is intended merely to provide some insights on the religiosity of African-Americans from Biblical to contemporary times. Hence, it is intended as a practical source on selective dimensions of Black Religiosity America rather than an historical analysis of this phenomenon.

INTRODUCTION

America is known as the melting pot because diversity of its immigrants to this "New Country". It has the Statue of Liberty to welcome immigrants to America. This nation, also, embodies the Horatio Alger's "Rags to Riches" Dream where an immigrant—through hard work, thriftiness, and persistence—can attain upward mobility.

America's population from the following sources: the English Colonists, the Native Americans (Indians) Subsequent European immigrants, and the Africans who were brought under duress and subjected to perpetual servitude, a system known as Slavery that started in Virginia in 1619 and ended by a Presidential Proclamation on January 1, 1863.

During that period of over Two Centuries, the Africans were sold at the auction block—a symbol of the activity still stands at Saint Augustine, Florida—subjected to an intensive a socialization designed to create docility; it included several prohibition such as discontinuation of speaking in their native tongue, no formal education, no religious, and total reliance on their plantation owner for instruction and directions. The new training and indoctrination was only partial successful for it could not erase the Slaves' belief in God and commitment to family. In those two areas, the Slaves started secret worshiping services held late at night and usually far from the Plantation owner's home. With respect to the family, the Slave mother would attend to her children late at night after having fulfilled her daily chores. It was within this context the she home schooled her children, without books, but relying of oral tradition that included precepts and religious ideas. A renown anthropologist characterized Africans as having an unusual capacity to learn by memorization, an example of which is telling stories. The writer, Joe Chandler Harris, successfully demonstrated this reality in his series on Uncle Remus.

It is in memory of the religious zeal maintained by an enslaved people that this collection of sermons was prepared. The intent is twofold, namely, to remind contemporary readers of the emphases that enslaved people placed on God as they coped with inhumane condition and, second, to challenge contemporary humanity to remember that God is yet on the throne and no longer is it prohibited to worship the Almighty God.

WHAT IS MAN?

"What is man, that thou art mindful of him"
(Ps. 8:4).

The question "What is man?" is historic and has been the focus of innumerable explanations along with speculations. In elementary biology, this question is answered by citing historical and anthropological data. With respect to taxonomy, man is placed into a species classification known as *Homo sapiens* and is located at the top of the animal world. While this theoretical information is both interesting and intriguing, it is radically different from the biblical account of humanity. Accordingly, the sermon for today will address this topic under the subject, What Is Man? The sermon will encompass the following three dimensions or concerns: the evolution of human knowledge; three different views on the origin of life; and the preferred response to the question, "what is man?"

Deviating from the usual format of background observations on the subject prior to the analysis of its dimension, the sermon will commence with the first objective, which encompasses a background. As earlier noted, the first concern is that the evolution of human knowledge.

The philosopher John Locke advanced the notion that at birth each individual's mind is like a blackboard with nothing written thereon. In the process of time, according to Locke, each person is exposed to human contacts, introduced to ideas, given formal training, and soon learns to think and to process information—all of which is symbolically written on the blackboard of the individual's mind. In the process of time, each person will have acquired values, perceptions, and preferences.

This learning process was also addressed by Emile Durkheim who theorized that an individual born and reared within a given cultural setting will soon commence to communicate, think, and act within the framework of that culture. In sum, this sketch of these two scholars supports the conclusion that human knowledge consists of varying rather than a single view. Additionally, these different perceptions ultimately led to specific areas of compartmentalized academic knowledge, three of which will be highlighted in the second phase of this sermon; they are philosophy, science, and religion.

It is readily admitted that the study of human knowledge encompasses innumerable areas or disciplines; hence, no claim is herein made that this sermon is exhaustive of disciplines. Instead, it is structured within the confines of three areas that offer responses to the question, "what is man?" The three areas are philosophy, science, and religion. In that order, the sermon will now explore some parameters of each view.

The pioneer philosophical response to this question was given by Thales, an early philosophical thinker who resided in the Aegean Sea area. He was impressed by water and observed that all forms of life seemed to have come out of the water. Thales, therefore, concluded that human life came out of the water. His view never received credence in the philosophical area later established by Socrates, Plato, and Aristotle. However, he should be recognized for having the curiosity to ponder the question, "what is man?"

This question was also a topic of concern in the area known as science. Probably the most controversial response was couched in the famous evolutionary theory of Charles Darwin. He asserted that over millions of years, humankind evolved from a primitive animal-like structure into a form known as *Homo erectus* (i.e., from crawling to walking as the form of movement). Darwin's view was consistent with earlier anthropological writings, one of which states, "from at least 6 to 3 million years ago, early humans combined apelike and humanlike ways of moving around." It must be noted that, despite Darwin's scholarship, his evolutionary theory of humanity was controversial and even the basis of a famous court case labeled The Scopes Monkey Trial. Since Theles and Darwin have been found inadequate to answer the question, "what is man?", attention will now be focused on the authentic source that provides the answer for this puzzling question. It is found in the discipline known as religion in which the Holy Bible is the recorded reference that contains the answer to the question.

Prior to presenting the religious response, it is deemed appropriate to briefly critique the areas of philosophy and science. Each of these disciplines contains essential information to enhance the intellectual status of humanity; however, both are inadequate to explain the origin and ultimate destiny of humankind. Philosophy can provide mental challenges through logic and dialogue, but it offers no definite plan for life after death. In a similar manner, science provides extensive information on plant and animal life, including methodologies to prolong their longevity; yet science is unable to extend life into infinity, nor can it provide any assurance of life after death.

Beloved, let us not shudder and grow sick at heart owing to the limitations of philosophy and science. Instead, let us embrace religion and its teachings as found in the Holy Bible. Therein is found the unequivocal answer to the question, "what is man?" The Bible asserts that God created man in his own image (Gen. 1:26); hence, human life did not come out of the water nor from a lower form of animal life. The biblical documentation is quite extensive in Psalm 8 within regard to the question in study. Therein it is noted he received divine visits, he is created a little lower than the angels, he is crowned with glory and honor, he is given dominion over the works of God's hands, and all things are under his feet (Ps. 8:4-6).

In closing, we as readers and hearers of this sermon should be thankful for our vast knowledge base and seek to access and utilize it properly (i.e., to learn, to properly utilize, to be helpful, and to embrace teachings and precepts contained in the Holy Bible). In terms of philosophy, we are privileged to speculate, and in terms of science, we are blessed to know. But in terms of religion, we are challenged to believe, encouraged to help, and reminded to wait upon the Lord and be of good courage. This must be our stance because we came not from the water, nor from a lower form of animal life; instead we are products of the handiworks of God. Amen.

THE SLAVES' RELIGIOUS EXPERIENCES

"And he said, Cursed be Canaan; a servant of servants he be unto his brethren"
(Gen. 9:25);

"Thou shall not kill…
Thou shall not steal"
(Ex. 20:13-15).

One of the restrictions placed on the newly arriving Africans for slavery in America was that of no organized religious activity. The initial justification for this prohibition was that the slaves were subhumans and had no soul; therefore, they needed no exposure to religion.

While being unaware of such an explanation, the slaves soon devised a method to hold secret worship late at night and away from their owners' houses. It became known as the Underground Church. The efficacy of this worship style required a coded form of communication to disseminate information regarding the time and place, and to describe the impressions of the services. In response to this need, the slaves evolved a system of communication known as the Negro Spirituals. The use and efficacy of the spirituals have been documented, and they became a part of the repertoire of performances, especially at black colleges and universities.

A few of the coded meanings included: "Satan" as an insensitive plantation owner; "King Jesus" as a listening, understanding, and somewhat humane plantation owner; "I could not hear nobody pray" was the monitor near the plantation owner's house to gauge the noise level from the Underground Church; "I felt like shouting when I come out the wilderness" was a response to describe the satisfaction derived from worshipping at the Underground Church; and "De gospel train is a coming" was a method to spread the word about the next Underground schedule to share of the emotional.

This Underground Church movement seems to have inspired a proactive stance against the institution of slavery starting in 1800. A religious leader, Gabriel Posser, attempted to engender an uprising against slavery in Virginia. As would be expected during those days, Posser was put to death. That death did not permanently eradicate ministerial leading in the call to end slavery. The next attempt to overthrow slavery was initiated by Denmark Vesay in South Carolina. His destiny was like that of Prosser's, but the rebellion was still alive as reflected in the action of Nat Turner in Virginia. He, like his two forerunners, was put to death.

The South, in recognizing the continuance of this religious effort to challenge, if not destroy, slavery, moved legislatively to ban all such endeavors; three southern states enacted codes to prohibit slaves from gathering in more than groups of ten for worship activities.

Recognizing the increasing spread of the abolition movement, there was a decline in the "no soul" view of slaves, and those southern states instituted a threefold modality to at least provide some options for slave worship. Those provisions were: slaves could hold worship but under the presence of a white monitor, and slaves could hold worship under the preaching of a white minister. This setting provided the ideal setting in which slaves could be subjected to a distorted view of their destiny according to the Bible. There were two frequently used Scriptures, one to justify slavery and the other to teach proper conduct to slaves. A frequently used Scripture to justify slavery was the account of Noah and his curse on Ham. This biblical episode is hardly adequate to justify Africans as being descendants of Ham's family line. With respect to proper slave conduct, two readings from the Decalogue were used, namely, "thou shall not kill" and "thou shall not steal" (Exodus 29:13-15).

The third alternative for slave worship was that of attending a white church but being seated in the balcony. That arrangement was often segmental for the slaves were excluded from the altar call and communion observation.

As these sinister tactics were being implemented, there was an emerging slave preacher whose name was John Jasper coming into the religious arena of slave religion. His transition from a slave field hand to a preacher is documented in a book entitled, John Jasper. According to that source, Jasper was converted at age twenty-five and was preaching at the time of Emancipation; he continued his calling after slavery; his vivid preaching—although filled with dialectic expressions—appealed to a vast number of listeners. Jasper was also in demand as a guest preacher. He left as a memorial a church built under his leadership; it is known as the Sixth Mount Zion Baptist Church in Richmond, Virginia. This writer had the privilege of visiting that church in July of 2009 and, upon talking with the pastor prior the morning worship, had the opportunity to "bring to light" a descendant of John Jasper who holds membership in that fellowship, but had never been recognized as a descendant of John Jasper.

While the emphasis in this message is focused on efforts by and reactions of slaves within the religious arena, it must be noted, however, that three different white responses occurred between 1800 and 1863. There was, first, an ongoing debate in the American Baptist over the question of slavery; the intensity of this controversy led to division in the American Baptist Convention.

The Southern States withdrew and formed in Southern Baptist Convention in 1845. The next initiative came with the Southern Methodist Church; it made provisions for Africans to have a separate worship with the Southern Methodist in 1870 the denomination was known as The African Methodist Church, a title that was changed in 1957 to The Christian Methodist Church. Thirdly, during slavery and several years after Emancipation, there occurred the Sunday School movement in the South; it was started for Slaves and conducted by Northern volunteers who were largely females.

In summation, the religious experiences of Slaves evolved through a series of stages that included: prohibition, the underground church, the Southern codes that provided three different modes for worship, the Sunday School Movement and, after Emancipation, the proliferation of denominations along with the beginning of church supported schools and colleges.

THE ETHIOPIAN EUNUCH

Acts 8:26-28
"And angel of the Lord spake unto Philip…
he arose (and met) a man of Ethiopia".

This Sunday is weekly day of worship for Christians throughout the world. Whereas some Sundays encompass a special focus like Mother's Day, for example, the Second Sunday in February has two additional focuses, namely: Race Relation Observation and the beginning of what Carter G. Woodson started as Negro History. That latter emphasis has been enlarged to include the entire month of February and is now known as Black History Month. This is also the month that encompasses the birth day of Abraham Lincoln and Frederick Douglas.

While both of these event are significant, the sermon today will be confined to the Black History emphasis. It has been entitled, **The Ethiopian Eunuch.** The sermon has been planned around three objectives, namely: to document the long history of Black participation in the history of Christianity; to implant a seed of racial pride in us as people of Color; and to stimulate thoughts on our self perception in this journey known as life.

In addition to its textual basis, the sermon will include two other sources for the topic of Blacks in the Bible; they are: <u>All the Men of the Bible</u>, by Herbert Lockyer and <u>The Black Presence in</u>

the Bible, by Walter Arthur McCray. These sources include an extensive listing of Blacks in the Bible, some of which are Moses' Wife, Joseph's Wife, Simon of Cyrena, Candace, and the Ethiopian Eunuch. While each of these persons is worthy of a character study, the sermon will be restricted to the Ethiopian Eunuch.

Prior to addressing the earlier identified objectives, attention will be focused on the Ethiopian Eunuch. This person lived during the 1st Century which was also the time of the Apostles. He was a native of an African area known as Ethiopia. That country was so named to designate the skin color of the inhabitants. In biblical archaeology, the area is labeled as Cush or the land of one of Noah's Sons. "Modern Ethiopia is an independent country occupying some 450, 000 square miles of Eastern Africa between Sudan and Somalia. The natives referred to Ethiopia as Abyssinia, or brotherhood. Let us keep this word, Abyssinia, in for it will appear again later in the sermon. Against this brief account of the Eunuch's native country, attention will now be focused on the earlier identified objectives, the first of which is to document the long history of Black participation in the history of Christianity. Even before the New Testament period, Blacks were involved in Old Testament Religion. Moses, author of the first five books of the Old Testament was married to a Black Woman. Joseph, the youngster sold into Egyptian slavery was married to a woman of color, Queen Candice who provided supplies for Solomon to construct the Temple was a woman of Color; one of the three wise men who visited the Christ Child was from Africa, Simon who was forced to bear the cross of Jesus was a man of color, and the Ethiopian Eunuch was a black man. Beloved, these are but a few people of color that lived during early Biblical history. Against this biblical background, let us turn to a gross historical distortion; it is that Caucasian, or White, argument that Slavery—despite its horrors—introduced people of color to Christianity. My friends, that argument is false as revealed by the same Bible that those people use; further, its falsity is disclosed by the denial and/restrictions that Plantation owners placed upon slave worship. In his book on the

Negro Church, Emanuel McCall, indicated that in 1832 Alabama, Georgia, and Virginia had enacted laws to prohibit Black gathering for religious services. Thirdly, this falsity of Slavery being the channel of Christianity for Black folk is reflected in philosophical history. Remembering that slavery started in 1619, let us life a citation from Morris Engels, History of Philosophy. It is the section where he documents the existence of a Black philosopher and theological, Saint Augustine, who lived from 354-430, long before slavery. This person of color was a prominent philosopher, write, and later became Bishop of the Catholic Church in Hippo, Africa. In sum, this synopsis of three factors has clearly shown that Christianity among people of color was not a by product of slavery. This incontrovertible fact leads to the second objective which is to <u>implant a seed of racial pride in us as people of Color.</u> From the time of Lynch's address given in Virginia on the making of a slave to contemporary subtle tactics, people of color have been humiliated, neglected, exploited, and even killed. Such dehumanizing efforts have lead to a mind set of insecurity, under reaction, and black on black assaults. The urgent need, in this connection, is for a change in the mind set of our people. How can this reversal be attained? Numerous are the existing procedures, however, our sermon will emphasize the one reflected by the Ethiopian Eunuch. In this connection, a brief profile of the Eunuch is deemed appropriate. The profile discloses that he was a man of color; he had been rendered incapable of reproducing and, therefore, known as the Eunuch. Despite these two problem areas, that individual was literate; hence he could read (Acts 8:28); he was a trust worthy person; he was treasurer for Queen Candace; he rode in a chariot; and possessed a copy of the Hebrew stroll, and he read during his spare time. The Eunuch, while being a person of great authority, had a spiritual yearning. Thus, he frequently read the sacred book of his time. When approached by Philip, the Eunuch inquired of him as to whom Esaiah was writing. After having listened to Philip, the Eunuch was converted and he request Philip to baptize him. The account of the Eunuch ended with him going on his way which was back to Ethiopia where, according to Biblical archeology, he established the first Church in Ethiopia and named it Abyssinia, Christian brotherhood. Friends, many years later some people of Ethiopia came to America and they established Churches and named them Abyssinia Baptist Church, the most famous being located in Harlem, New York. In sum, this profile clearly shows that being of color should be no categorical block to education, morality, self-respect and Christian Service. This fact leads to the third, and final objective of the sermon, namely—to stimulate thought on our purpose on this journey known as life. Beloved, and especially our young people, we are people of color so let us remember the biblical question—Can the Ethiopian change his color or the leopard its spots. In this regard, we must never let our mind concentrate on color and its liabilities; instead, we must learn to read, to think, and to be proud of our accomplishments. While there are many obstacles on our pathway, we must never shutter and grow sick. Instead, we must familiarize ourselves with books, including the Bible. As we become more serious and prayerful about our future, the Lord will send a way maker in to our life; he did it for the Ethiopian Eunuch and that person was thoroughly blessed. He rejoiced in giving his life to Jesus; he went back to his country and established a Church; and his legacy has been recorded in the annals of time. Friends, we may never hold an extremely powerful office; we may never become financially wealthy; we may never establish a church; we may never have a building named in our honor. But all of us can be respectable people of color; we can develop an appreciation for knowledge; we can display moral, ethical, and humanitarian values; we can embrace the principles of Christianity; and we can give our live over to Christ Jesus. Do you catch the vision; have you accepted Christ and will you remain on this Christian journey for the long haul?

AN OUTREACH LEGACY OF A BLACK CHURCH

Joshua 4:4-6
". . . take you up every man of you a stone upon his shoulder..."

The system of slavery in 1619 and continued until the Presidential Proclamation January1,1863. It was based upon trafficking and sale of Africans to plantation owners. Upon being purchased, the enslaved people were subjected to a rigorous indoctrination process; it concluded a discontinuation of their native language, no formal training of offsprings, and no gathering for religious purposes.

The slaves continued to maintain their belief in God so they held prayer meetings in their huts and later started the Under ground Church. That enduring religious commitment continued after slavery as reflected in the establishing of churches along with outreach functions that included schools, colleges, and burial societies.

Against these background observations, let us now turn to the purpose for which we are here assembled. It is that of recognizing a significant outreach of this St. Paul Baptist Church, here in Kinder, LA.—i.e., serving as the arena of educational access for people of color. This Church is to be commended for that worthy cause. Obviously, it was committed to both the religious and the educational welfare of its members and others within the geographical area. That successful undertaking has certainly become a legacy of this Church. In recognition of this reality and sensing the new directions of churches, a decision was made to use as a subject this afternoon—**An Outreach Legacy of the Black Church.** This subject is an expression of a fervent concern I have for the preservation of the Black Church. It reflects my many years of experience in the church as a member, an usher, a theological student, a pastor, and a seminary dean.

It is an unfortunate fact that the black church has been largely focused on other worldly prospects. Admittedly, salvation is the core of the Christian religion and the church must proclaim this good news. Owing to societal inequalities imposed on certain groups of people, the Black Church came to their aid. That type of activity was worldly rather than other worldly oriented. In attempting to fill the void of neglect, the church begins to fulfill outreach functions. The scope of needs include, food, clothing, counseling, housing, and educational opportunities. It was in response to the last area—education—is where this church symbolically stepped up to the plate and belted a grand slam home run. Accordingly, we are today saluting you for a meaningful educational outreach that stands as a legacy for this church, parish, state, and nation.

This episode is a lucid example of what a church can do to enhance the spiritual and social welfare of its members. It merited inclusion in the annuals of investigations on black people in America. It ranks with events documented in research on blacks between 1900 and 1950. The so called grandfather of research on American blacks was the late William E. B. DuBois was a pioneer Black scholar whose research included studies on the Black Church, In his book entitled, <u>The Souls of Black Folk,</u> Dr. DuBois wrote about the impact of religion on the black personality. Another researcher, E. Franklin Frazier reported that blacks in

Chicago often started worship centers in abandoned stores; he referred to those locations as "Store front" Churches. Both of those scholars conducted extensive research on the black church and they found it anchored, molded, and energized the black personality It must be noted, however, that the black preacher was the guiding force in the black church. He was the one who provided religious interpretations of daily living; he was the one who encouraged blacks to persevere; and he was the one whom white society viewed with suspicion. Commenting on this semi distrust of black preachers, Emmanuel McCall, in a book entitled, Black Church: Lifestyles, . . . wrote (The paradox is that... black preaching and worship were" viewed with distrust by whites; hence, they felt that the worship was revolionary). Such a view was ironic since the slave indoctrination included prohibition of future use of the native language, separation from tribal groups, and denial of educational opportunities. Yet in the early 1800's, the white fear was crystalized by the efforts of three slave preachers. The first was Gabriel Prosser who in 1800 sought to overthrow slavery in Virginia; the second was Denmark Vassey who in 1822 led an unsuccessful uprising in Charleston, S.C. and the third was Nat Turner who in 1831 led a bloody revolt in Southampton, Virginia. These religious insurrectionists were put to death.

Two years later, Alabama became the first state to prohibit slave gathering for religious purposes. In response to the new laws, the slaves started a worship form known as the underground church. It was held in the cotton field, in a slave cabin, or under a shade tree during lunch break.

As the underground churches became more structured, their so called unlearned and unlettered preachers issued a call for Sunday School teachers who would help slave children learn to read, write, and spell. Henry Adams organized the first church sponsored school which was held in the church facility. In 1856, the African Methodists established Wilberforce University. That act started a chain reaction of denominational schools, colleges, and universities. (name, if deemed appropriate)

Not so highly spotlighted, documented, nor acclaimed were the many little churches that established grade schools. Yet such little schools became feeder sources for the colleges and universities.

In support of this assertion, I call attention to my educational journey. It started in a one teacher elementary school, located at the family church, with the same name as the church. The name, Saint Stephen was used to denote the church and, also, the school. My experience was not an isolated event for church sponsored schools were established in rural areas through the Old South. These institutions functioned on a meager budget and little recognition by the public school officials. Yet the little school pupils were nurtured by parental support, encouraged by church members, and impelled by a dream of rising about the ruts of inequality. Hence, they preserved dreaming the impossible dreams, mentally climbing the unconquerable mountains, and swimming the turbulent sea of opposition.

Friends, the story of minority pupil struggling to obtain an education and the role of the church in blazing the trail must never be forgotten. This church's outreach is worthy of being enshrined into the annals of educational history. It is a legacy that is comparable to the crossing of Jordan when Joshua instructed the religious leaders to collect twelve stones from the bottom of Jordan for future reference. They inquired why these stones and Joshua replied that you can tell them of the miracles that God performed on their behalf. In a similar manner, this event today is a contemporary illustration of the Joshua command. It requires no gathering of stones, but the granting of recognition as an historical cite does serve as a reminder of a church sponsored educational legacy here in the Parish of Allen, the town of Kinder in the State of LA.

The St. Paul Baptist Church of that town served as St. Paul/Morehead Public School for children of color until 1945. In 2006, it was recipient of The Historic Preservation plaque.

THE SAGA OF BLACK PREACHING IN AMERICA

Colonization of the new world that would ultimately be known as America occurred in 1607, the King James Version of the Bible was released in 1611, and slavery was started in America in 1619. Since the colonists were in pursuit of freedom, including religion, and they used the King James Version of the Bible, it was ironic that they embraced slavery.

Immediately upon the start of slavery, there were strict codes imposed to transform the African captives into docile slaves. Among the measures were: no further use of the native language, no formal education, and no religious gatherings. To an extent, the plantation owners were successful with language and educational prohibitions, but they failed to stamp out religion among the slaves. Within a short time after their arrival, the slaves started a secret worship at night that was later known as the underground church. Within that setting was an unofficial religious leader designated by the title, preacher.

Since that time until this 21st Century, there have been and will forever be Black Preachers, a decision was made to use as a subject for the occasion tonight, The Saga of Black Preaching in America. Admittedly, the word saga—as used herein is taken out of its epistemological context, but is does follow the format of a narrative similar of Iceland where emphasis was placed on a legendary individual of event. Accordingly, it is herein submitted that Black Preaching in America complies with the schema of a saga. Accepting the tenability of this premise, the following dimensions will anchor the subject earlier delineated, Black preaching during slavery, Black preaching from Emancipation to the Civil Rights Movement, and Black Preaching during the 21th Century.

Prior to addressing these components of the subject, attention will be focused on the plantation owners use of Bible to justify slavery.

The white preachers sought to justify slavery by two approaches; the first one was the declare that the slaves had no soul and, therefore, needed no religious experiences. Their second scheme was to preach and teach that slavery was a biblical curse that dated back to Noah where he placed a curse on his son, Canaan (Gen.25). That interpretation is in error because Canaan's land included the people of India and none of them were enslaved.

Another consideration, prior to analyzing the foci of this address is the word preaching. As used with the biblical context, preaching denotes the act of expounding on a word or theme anchored by a scriptural reference. As reflected in Jesus' announcement of his preaching obligation, it requires a calling and an anointing (Lk. 4:18).

With this background, attention will be focused on the three earlier identified components of the subject—the first one being—black preaching during slavery. As earlier noted, that type of action was prohibited. However, the underground church was very much alive. For over two Centuries, the slaves participated in that type of worship setting. In the early part of the 19th Century, the underground church became proactive under the leadership of three different persons, each of whom who sought to overthrow slavery; they were Gabriel Posser (1800), Richmond, VA.; Denmark Vesey, 1822, in Charleston, S.C.; and Nat Turner,

1831 in South Hampton, VA. As would be expected, each of those persons was put to death. To advert such future efforts, three Southern States (Al., MS., GA) made it unlawful for slaves or free Negroes to gather in ten or more for religious services, unless it occurred under a white monitor or preacher.

A few later, there occurred a rare instance in which a slave converted his master and was eventually given freedom to preach the gospel; his name was John Jasper.

Prior to closing this first period, Black preaching during slavery, brief consideration will be given to a burial practice in Stapelo Island, GA. The natives are known as Gullah people. Years ago, the mode of disposing a deceased person was to place the body in an open rice field where it could be consumed by buzzards. Those people held a memorial in the form of a ring shout. It consisted of forming a circle within which a person was dressed in white, held up his arms, made motion with them to symbolize the buzzard soon to approach and consume the body. That person was known as the buzzard. Since that time, the term buzzard has been used to denote a preacher who attends funeral only to participate in the repast.

The next period was known as the Post Slavery Era; it commenced prior to the end of slavery as reflected in the founding of Wiberforce University. That institution, founded in 1856, was intended for the education of Negroes—the title used then. Immediately after the end of slavery in 1865, there followed the establishment of denominations and they commenced to start colleges and seminaries for former slaves and free Negroes. Some of the church supported schools were: Allen University, Morris Brown College, Livingstone College, Arkansas Baptist College, and Virginia Theological Seminary—to name but a few.

During this second period, the Church assumed a variety of outreach functions, one of which was the Pall Burial Society. An additional indication of this early history is reflected on the back of funeral programs where pall burials are listed.

It was also during this time that several religious initiatives occurred, some of which were: one denominational group, The Baptist, in 1895 organized the National Baptist Convention in Atlanta, Georgia. USA was organized in Atlanta, Georgia in 1895. Although denominational and/or private bible colleges and seminaries were established during this second period, there were many committed preachers who possessed limited formal education. However, there was more emphasis placed on education within the Methodist than in the Baptist Denomination. Fortunately, that differential commenced to be less conspicuous during the third period as presented in this address. It commenced during the early 1920's and was characterized, first, by the cultist movement of Father Divine, the Back to Africa movement of Marcus Garvey, Garvey, the Pentecostal Movement under the leadership of Bishop Charles H. Mason, and the Muslim faith perpetrated by Elijah who changed his name to Elijah Mahammad.

Approximately twenty five years later, the black religious movement treaded into a new outreach area known as the Civil Rights Movement. It soon launched several black preachers into the national spotlight; some of them were Martin Luther King, Jr., Ralph D. Abernathy, Fred Shuttleworth, Andrew Young, and Jesse Jackson.

The scope of that movement undergirded much of the religious social pro stance during the remainder of the Twentieth Century. Although its thrust continued into the current century, there is a frightening trend that is alien to the movement; it is known as the mega church phenomenon.

Accordingly, black preaching is being lured from sound biblical preaching to ideologies that include the full gospel, the not for profit economic enterprises, and the electronic church modality.

Beloved, the closing challenge echoes aloud needs that include:

    a.   the need for formal bible college and seminary education

b. the need to know and preach the original gospel for it is complete, so no need for a so call—Full Gospel
c. avoid seeking a mega church and offer instead mega service regardless of the size of membership
d. remember your obligation is to seek and save those who are lost
e. be guided by Paul's instruction to Timothy for your preaching guidelines.

CHASING THE MIRAGE OF EQUALITY

I was both surprised and honored to learn of having been selected as speaker for this Annual Occasion. As I recall, this program has always included renown theologians, ecclesiastical giants, governmental officials, and other prestigious individuals. While recognizing the economic meltdown, it now seems that the oratorical arena has become a victim of that reality, a fact evident in the decision to select me as speaker. Yet, the determination has been made, the program is in session, and it is now time for the address. To this end, I have chosen to speak from the subject—Chasing the Mirage of Equality.

The Emancipation Day Program elicits various memories and/or emotions. Many speakers use the occasion to engender quasi hostilities between the two dominant races, an intent that I vehemently refute. Instead, the approach today will focus on enlightenment on the past, awareness of the present, and preparation for the future.

Since there are various anchors for addresses, it is deemed appropriate to identify three of them used on an Emancipation Day observation. The most frequently used one is the chronological approach. Essentially, it is largely a listing of persons who were prominent during the period of slavery. Secondly, there is the adversarial approach. It seeks to create and/or intensify suspicion, hostility, and disdain between racial groups. Thirdly, used in this address, is the theme approach. It is holistic and, as such, examines the spirit of the time, the prevailing outlook, and the societal behaviors. Using this orientation, three themes will be analyzed, namely: The misconception regarding Lincoln's Proclamation of Emancipation; selective episodes of the slave saga; and problems along with challenges for contemporary African Americans.

Prior to examining these three dimensions, brief attention will be focused on the word, mirage. This concept refers to an optical effect sometimes seen at sea, on the desert, or over a hot paved highway. It gives the impression of a pool of water or a mirror effect of waving light. The mirage always remains out of distance of the viewer as noted in a moving automobile; as the automobile moves faster so does the mirage. In a similar manner equality for African Americans—to a large extent—continues to be a mirage. Against this verity, attention will now be focused on the earlier delineated themes, the first of which is <u>The Misconception regarding Lincoln's Proclamation of Emancipation.</u> Many persons of my grandfather's generation—when permitted to vote—identified themselves with the Democratic party, but openly stated that they felt obligated to vote Republican because Lincoln gave them freedom. It must be noted, however that Lincoln was no humanitarian for the cause of slavery; he was instead a shred politician who sought a method to preserve the Union and punish those Confederate states who were reluctant to return to the union. The following quote will substantiate this assertion.

> On this day in 1863, Abraham Lincoln signs the Emancipation Proclamation. Attempting to stitch together a nation mired in a bloody civil war, Abraham Lincoln made a last-ditch, but carefully calculated, decision regarding the institution of slavery in America.

By the end of 1862, things were not looking good for the Union. The Confederate Army had overcome Union troops in significant battles and Britain and France were set to officially recognize the Confederacy as a separate nation. In an August 1862 letter to New York Tribune editor Horace Greeley, Lincoln confessed "my paramount object in this struggle is to save the Union, and it is not either to save or to destroy slavery." Lincoln hoped that declaring a national policy of emancipation would stimulate a rush of the South's slaves into the ranks of the Union army, thus depleting the Confederacy's labor force, on which the Southern States depended to wage war against the North.

Having documented Lincoln's view on slavery, the next theme in this address is that of a partial sketch of prominent slaves during that inhuman period in American History. Admittedly, this dimension will have to be both brief and eclectic in view of the countless individuals worthy of being included in this sketch. An extensive document on the slave experiences can be found in Up from Slavery, by John Hope Franklin. However, just a few of those individuals are referenced herein. Gabriel Posser, Demark Vasey, and Nat Turner were three slave preachers who sought to disrupt slavery; they were all put to death. There was Harriet Tubman who started the underground railroad and SoJourner Truth, an abolitionist, whose best-known extemporaneous speech on racial inequalities, Ain't I a Woman?, was delivered in 1851 at the Ohio Women's Rights. The list, also, includes Dred Scott—a slave who sued for freedom—but the Supreme Court of MO.—ruled against him stating that a slave is property and it can be move from state to state without a change in status. That ruling was issued March 6, 1857. But within four years later, slavery would be ended by a Presidential order (January 1, 1863). In response to the Proclamation, the slave abolitionists, Frederick Douglass, referenced that document in an address that he delivered at the Cooper Institute in New York on February 6, 1863. He said,

We are all liberated by this proclamation. Everybody is liberated. The white man is liberated, the black man is liberated, the brave men now fighting the battles of their country against rebels and traitors are now liberated, and may strike with all their might, even if they do hurt the Rebels, at their most sensitive point. [Applause.] I congratulate you upon this amazing change—the amazing approximation toward the sacred truth of human liberty.

At this point, the focus of this address will encompass a quantum from the 1860's to the 21th Century where the third, and final, dimension of this subject will be addressed. It is <u>The Problems and Challenges for Contemporary African Americans.</u>

Admittedly, our pathway to equality has been impaired by numerous external forces that started with slavery, continued with segregation, token integration, changing legal codes, and imposing elevated standards for admission to the educational arena. While these sinister codes and actions are not of our making, there does exist a plethora of problems emanating from us. Poetically, it phenomenon is like unto the utterance, "The fault dear Brutus is not within the stars, but we the underlings...". In this regard, it is herein asserted that we are the creators and perpetrators. The array of our problems helps to reinforce the mirage that eludes equality. No attempt is herein made to prioritize them; instead, a mere listing, with brief comments, will be given. The racially endemic problems include:

1. Black pathology sustains white capitalism. This word, pathology, refers to societal problems that include—but not limited to—crime, delinquency, lethargy, robbery, home invasions—to mention but a few examples. This reality sets in motion the police department, the legal core, the court system, the probation.

2. The underground economy—this expression denotes the drug culture, prostitution, gang activity, and street vendors for the white suppliers. Those apprehended for the violations necessitate the earlier reference so called justice system into action.
3. The rapid proliferation of gang. Again, white capitalism benefits from this anti social action.
4. Black on black crime. It is a truism that blacks are more inclined to kill within their race than in the white group. This action is another facet for white capitalism; however, the black funeral directors get a little of the economic finality.
5. Multi generational lethargy—this is a family pattern in which the grandmother was a welfare recipient, the daughter followed the mother, and now the young daughter is with child. Such behavior is a sad commentary on domestic life.

These are but a few of the problems from within our race that heighten the mirage between our race and full equality.

Although difficult may seem an alternation, it is herein submitted that a positive change can be achieved. It will not come easy or from blaming others; instead, its realization is embedded in the following challenges: First, there must be a moral reawakening; one that will emphasize self respect and the recognition that personal behavior should be an highly esteemed objective. Secondly, there must be an ethical resurgence, one of a type that promotes fair play, good will, honesty, and respect for the rights of others. Thirdly, there is the need for educational experiences not just for children, but parents and/or other adults with the household. Fourthly, our group is in dire need of a religious renaissance, a term in history used to denote the rebirth of a refined way of life. It became the guiding principle as civilization moved from the Dark Ages to the period of Enlightenment. The searching question is—where can the basis for the Enlightenment be found? Is it in history—no there are too many pages; it is in philosophy—no there are too many speculation; is it in science—no there are to many theories; is it in statistics—no there are too many theorems; is it in literature—no there is too much poetry; is it in a GPS—no there are too many satellites. But wait, don't shutter and grow sick at heart because has been handed down to us as noted in the Book of Books, Heb. 12:1-2 ". . . let us lay aside every weight, and sin which doeth so easily beset us, and let us run with patience the race that is set before us. Looking unto Jesus the author and finisher of our faith. So in closing, drop those four weights and to ". . . run with patience the race that is set before us looking unto Jesus the author and finisher of our faith…" (Heb. 12:1)

THE AMERICAN BLACK DILEMMA

In 1835, the Frenchman, Alexis de Tocqueville, published his highly acclaimed book entitled, Democracy in America. He characterized Americans as being fascinated by and in constant pursuit of material goals with little commitment for ethical and moral values.

In 1944, the Swedish sociologist—Gunnar Myrdal—st udied Americans from the perspective of adherence to the Democratic Creed and their treatment of—quoting Myrdal—the American Negroes. Myrdal hypothesized that two response patterns existed in the white community with respect to the nonwhite population. First, there were those whites who fully embraced the democratic creed and, therefore, accepted integration. In contrast, there were others who rejected the democratic creed and readily championed segregation. However, between those two polarities, Myrdal found that the majority of white Americans were baffled by both options and, therefore, sought to comply with the normative response within the setting in which they found themselves. Myrdal labeled that phenomenon as An American Dilemma.

While being less well known than those scholars, this speaker for today's Black History Event has no trepidation regarding personal competency to look at American from the stance of its Black population using as a subject—The American Black Dilemma.

Black Religiosity: A Biblical and Historical Perspective

Prior to exploring components of this topic, it is deemed appropriate to highlight the origin of Black History Month. The organizer of this occasion was Carter G. Woodson, professor, writer, and founder of the CW Institute. He labeled it as Negro History Week and scheduled for the second week in February; it embraced the birthdays of Abraham Lincoln and Frederick Douglas. That week was set aside to remember the unethical and inhumane system of slavery, to call attention to contributions of Negroes, the term used at that time, to America, and to instill within the slave descendants a desire to fully participate in the American society whose affluence was wrought on the backs of slaves. The name and duration of this event was changed and modified after the death of Dr. Martin Luther Junior; it became known as Black History and was lengthened to encompass the entire month of February.

Against this brief sketch on the origin and title of this program for which we are assembled, the emphasis will be directed to the subject, earlier specified, The American Black Dilemma. To keep this presentation in perspective, the word—dilemma—will again be defined. It refers to a situation in which two opposing polarities exist and the individual must chose one while being guided, hopefully, by some ethical standard and humanitarian ideology. With this operational definition of dilemma, attention will now be focused on the American Black Dilemma. The presentation will be restricted to six dimensions, or in computer terminology, six windows; namely: de socialization of the slaves, miscegenation among the races, religion with the slave population, legal anomalies involving slaves, the post slave outreaches, and the pathway ahead.

Each of these parameters will now be addressed in the earlier delineated order. The institution of slavery in America commenced in 1619. Ironically, it started in the Colony of Virginia, the same located where 12 years earlier, 1607, colonization of the New World had started.

Owing to the whites' fear of insurrection attempts by the slaves, they instituted a rigorous process of de socialization the slaves and instilling within the enslaved a "a slave mentality". This process encompassed actions that including purchasing slaves from different tribal setting, prohibiting the use of the African language, and denial of religious worships.

The next issue was that of sexuality involving whites and slaves. Initially, it was assumed that sensuality would involved only white men and slave women; hence, the rule became that a child born from such an encounter would have the race of its mother—the slave mother. But an unanticipated reality soon followed. It seemed that some white females were curious about fables involving slave males; hence, their proclivity was to investigate and, nature being completely democratic, functioned in accordance with biological normality. Accordingly, the offspring to the white woman posed a problem for racial identity. In response to that dilemma, a code was enacted known as the 1/8 clause that stated, irrespective to a child's color, it would be label as a Negro by confession or affidavit. Initially, the Southern States used locally formulated rules to cope with this problem. As the number of such births increased, some states took aggressive measures against both the child and mother. Maryland, in 1664, ordered such an interracial child to be a slave as was its father and the white mother would be subjected to slavery for the rest of her life.

As the problem of miscegenation was becoming normalized, another one was in the fomenting; it stemmed from religious activities within the slave population. A discussion of that problem, religion, leads to the third dimension of The American Black Dilemma.

Although slave gathering for religious purposes was prohibited, the slaves devised a secret type of assembling known as the underground Church. In the process of time, the underground church assumed a proactive stance. Under the leadership of three different preachers at different times and locations, efforts were made to confront the slave system. The three mystic preachers were Gabriel Posser, Denmark Vesey, and Nat Turner. As would be expected each one was put to death. In response to possible future attempts, three Southern States: GA., MS., and AL. enacted anti religious codes encompassed three provisions: no more than ten slaves could hold worship; where more than ten slaves held worship there had to be a white monitor, and, thirdly, slaves could worship with the white population, but had to sit in the balcony.

Those Southern State Codes were forerunners to a ruling by the U.S. Supreme Court ruling on the legal status slaves. An examination of that case constitutes the fourth dimension of The American Black Dilemma which is a legal ruling on rights of slaves. Dred Scott sued unsuccessfully in the State of Illinois since his master had carried him from a slave to a non slave state. The litigation ended in the US Supreme Court where, under the leader ship of Chief Justice Roger B. Taney, himself a slave owner in Maryland, wrote the opinion. Essentially, it stated that slaves are property and property can be carried any place in the United States with a change or loss of status. was now in a non-slave state. The case was known as Dred Scott vs. Sanford and the year was 1857.

The last window is more the post slavery response to freedom after enactment of the 13th, 14th, and 15th Amendments to the Constitution, often called the Black Amendments. The newly freed people had no structured social organizations to fulfilled their individual and collective needs. It was in response to this void that the Negro Church—the designation at that time—assumed an extensive outreach programs. Scholars that include Frazier, DuBois, Franklin, and Fitts—concurred that the Negro Church outreaches became the source by which the former slaves were slowly made the transition from bondage to freedom.

Without question, the educational outreach was the most essential task assumed by the Negro Church. Although Wiberforce University was founded before the end of slavery, the plethora of church supported school, colleges and seminaries were established after 1865. A few of the institutions established during this church educational outreach efforts were: Shaw University, Leland University, Benedict College, Bishop College, Kentucky Normal and Theological Institute, Selma University, Arkansas Baptist College, and Virginia Theological Seminary—these and several other institutions were organized between 1865 and 1890.

In forming closure on The American Black Dilemma, it has be noted that the slave system, while enslaving former free people, had an array of unanticipated problems for the plantation owners. This address has analyzed five dimensions of the dilemma: de socialization, miscegenation, religion, legalities, post slavery outreaches, and the last one being the pathway ahead. This one embodies a two fold set of challenges; one for the Black population and the other for the White population. In that order, the Black population

1. must rise above welfare dependency
2. must refrain from the underground economy of drugs, prostitution, breaking and entering, and robbery
3. must eradicate the phenomenon known as Black pathology, an expression that encompasses the multiplicity of anti social behaviors. Admittedly, the American economy benefits from this pathology:' doctors, lawyers, dentists, the welfare network, the justice system and yes, the mortuary industry
4. must develop an affinity for formal education even beyond the high school level.

And now to the white population—

1. Remember your group started this problem for our ancestors were surviving in Africa and hardly knew anything about America

2. You must discard the practice of stereotyping the Black population, this tendency is being expanded to include racial profiling.
3. You must confront your latent racial negative attitudes
4. You must recognize that we are confronting a global reality in which the prestige of our nation is under scrutiny.

Let all of us remember that where there is unity there is strength even with demographic heterogeneity.

EPILOGUE

The Africans experiences in America were unique from all other immigrants to this country; it was that of slavery! In this writer's opinion, this system was man's inhumanity to humanity (enslaved Africans) short of genocide. Despite the horrors of servitude during two and one-half Centuries (1619-1863), the descendants of slaves, commenced a new life style as freed people. They were, yet, greatly challenged by the demands of independence. In attempted to cope with the new expectation of freedom, they sought to reestablish their often disjointed family, to establish churches, to organize schools, to start religious bible colleges, set up self help agencies—pall burial societies under the aegis of church to assist with burial expenses. Later, the freed people would start newspapers and insurance companies.

In sum, the former slaves were dedicated to and sustained by the family, the church, and their schools. Probably, the most sustaining force was their belief in and commitment to their Judeo Christian Religion, a fact demonstrated by their secret worship in the underground Church during the period of slavery. It is in memory of and tribute to the unwavering faith that sustained our African Ancestors in God who would on day deliver them as was the case with the Ancient Israel that this collection of sermons was prepared.

EGSJ.

SUGGESTED READINGS

1. The King James Version of the Bible, Broadman and Holman Publishers.
2. Cone, James. <u>Black Liberation Theology.</u> (NPR).
3. Costen, Melva Wilson. 1993. <u>African Amer ican Christian Worship.</u> Nashville: Abingdon Press.
4. DuBois, W.E.B. 1903. <u>The Souls of Black Folk.</u> A.C. McClung @Company.
5. Frazier, Edward Franklin. 1939. <u>The Negro Family in the United States.</u> University of Notre Dame Press.
6. Holly, Alonzo, (Reprinted in 1991). <u>God and the Negro.</u> National Baptist Publishing Board.
7. McCall, Emmanuel L. 1986. <u>Black Church Life Styles.</u> Nashville: Broadman Press.

ABOUT THE AUTHOR

Eugene G. Sherman, Jr. is professor emeritus of sociology from Albany State University in Albany, Georgia. His Academic credentials include five earned and two honorary degrees. In addition to his teaching assignments (sociology, gerontology, thanatology, religion and philosophy) he held administrative positions that included Chairman of the Division of Social Sciences, Chair of the Sociology Department, Acting Chair of History and Political Science, and Acting Chair of the College of Arts and Sciences. While discharging his university assignments, he established the Institutional First Baptist Church in 1971 where he continues to pastor; he was also Executive Dean of the Albany Center of Bethany Divinity College and Seminary (Dothan, AL) 1988-2011 when he retired. Since June of 2007, he has posted his weekly sermons on his website, www.biblicalechoes02.com before preaching them the following Sunday. Dr. Sherman has been widowed since the passing of his wife, Dr. Dolores E. Sherman, December 15, 2008. They had no children.

CPSIA information can be obtained
at www.ICGtesting.com
Printed in the USA
BVHW081101160922
647219BV00008B/292